AMAZON ADVENTURE

HOW TINY FISH ARE SAVING THE WORLD'S LARGEST RAINFOREST

WRITTEN BY **SY MONTGOMERY**

PHOTOGRAPHS BY **KEITH ELLENBOGEN**

HOUGHTON MIFFLIN HARCOURT
Boston New York

FOR DR. MILLMOSS,
IN MEMORY OF SALLY —S.M.

TO MY NIECE, MAYA, WHOSE LOVE
OF NATURE IS BOUNDLESS —K.E.

The text type was set in Latienne.
The display type was set in Populaire and Belta.

Library of Congress Cataloging-in-Publication Data is on file.
ISBN 978-0-544-35299-5

Manufactured in China
SCP 10 9 8 7 6 5 4 3 2 1
4500646738

TABLE OF CONTENTS

The crowns of drowned trees form
islands along the river margins.

CHAPTER 1
LITTLE FISH, GIANT JUNGLE

It's the planet's richest ecosystem, where a butterfly's wing can grow as big as your hand and five hundred species, from frogs to insects, can be found on a single flower. The Amazon basin—the 2,670,000 square miles drained by the Amazon River and its many tributaries—is the world's largest jungle, an area as big as the lower forty-eight U.S. states, the same size of the face of the full moon. Jaguars hunt in the shade of two-hundred-foot-tall trees; pink dolphins, who the local people claim have magic powers, swim in the rivers. New species discovered here in the last decade include a tarantula striped like a tiger, a bald parrot, a vegetarian piranha, and a monkey who purrs like a kitten.

This huge, ancient rainforest is essential to the planet. Because its trees provide a full fifth of the world's oxygen, it's considered "the lungs of the world." Yet it all could vanish—and soon. Each year, mining, clear-cutting, burning, and cattle ranching destroy

The MV *Iracema*, one of two riverboats carrying the Project Piaba team on its adventure.

an area of Amazon forest twice the size of the city of Los Angeles.

Luckily, beneath the glassy surface of its rivers live dozens of species of tiny, beautiful fish whose powers may be even greater than those of the mysterious pink dolphin or the mighty jaguar. These shy fish—so small the locals call them all *piaba* (pee-AH-bah), which roughly translates to "small fry" or "pip-squeak"—just might be able to save the Amazon.

How? We're on our way to find out.

We're traveling by riverboat from the port of Manaus up Brazil's Río Negro, one of the two main arteries that join to form the Amazon River. Our destination, 307 miles to the north, is Barcelos, a town of twenty-five thousand. Each year, fishermen come here from miles around, bringing some forty million of these small, colorful tropical fish that they caught in their forest communities. From Barcelos, the fish will be shipped to Manaus, and from there to public and home aquarium tanks around the world.

But wait: Capturing and exporting wild animals from their natural habitat sounds like a terrible idea—doesn't it?

Our host, Scott Dowd, agrees. "That's exactly what *I* thought when I first came here," he explains from aboard the deck of our boat, the MV *Dorinha*. A big man with a silvery beard and twinkling blue eyes, Scott knows better now. Today he eagerly admits, "I couldn't have been more wrong!"

Scott vividly recalls his first trip up the Río Negro. It was 1991. He was twenty-four years old, and he had teamed up with a prominent professor from the Federal University of Amazonas in Brazil, Dr. Ning Labbish Chao, to charter a boat with ten other fish enthusiasts. Thrilled to be in the green heart of the rainforest, Scott loved watching red and yellow macaws streak across the sky; he loved sleeping in a hammock on the boat at night and waking to the growling roars of howler monkeys in the morning. But mainly he came for the fish.

Today he is senior aquarist with the New England Aquarium in Boston, in charge of twelve thousand fish, frogs, snakes, and turtles in its Freshwater Gallery. He's always been, as he puts it, a "fish nerd." He started keeping fish tanks before he was ten. And, like just about any kid who keeps a freshwater fish tank, many of his first pet fish were species native to the tea-colored waters of the Río Negro.

A pair of blue and gold macaws.

Scott Dowd, at home in the dark waters of the Rio Negro.

An adult dwarf pike cichlid.

The river water here is stained dark from tannins—natural chemicals that come from plants whose leaves fall into these pure waters. The tannins make the water acidic. "The waters are pristine—but it's a hard place to make a living if you're a fish," Scott says. Adaptation to the difficult conditions here has sculpted beautiful and bizarre fish such as cardinal tetras, who glow in the dark with neon stripes of electric red and hyacinth blue; marbled hatchetfish, who can fly out of the water to escape predators; and splash tetras, who spawn on the wet undersides of overhanging tree leaves to keep their eggs safe (the male lurks below in the water for days and uses his fins to throw water up at the eggs to keep them moist). Scott could not wait to visit Barcelos, the town from which so many of the fish he had kept as a child and tended at the New England Aquarium had been shipped.

But when his group finally arrived at the town, Scott was horrified. The riverfront was jammed with men in dugout and plank canoes. They had come from an area of rainforest the size of Pennsylvania, bringing hand-woven plastic-lined baskets full of living fish that would fill hundreds of eight-gallon tubs, each containing eight hundred fish. There were so many tubs that they covered the entire bottom floor of the eighty-foot ferry that was docked at the pier, readying to return to Manaus.

"My knee-jerk reaction was, 'This is out of control!'" Scott remembers. "I thought, we shouldn't be taking wildlife from the rainforest; we should be farming them!"

But back then, he says, he didn't realize what would happen if the fishermen simply left these fish alone.

In the Amazon rainforest there are only two seasons: wet and dry. During the wet season, which corresponds to North America's winter and spring, it rains every day and the forest floods. Trees stand up to their crowns in water. People build houses on stilts, or on pontoons so they can float. Kids don't take a bus to school—they take a boat. Then, in the dry season, during our summer and fall, the water level drops—sometimes more than thirty feet. Nearly ninety percent of the small fish here are stranded, doomed in drying puddles.

It's the start of the dry season when most of the fishing for piaba takes place. For the fish who are captured, it's like a rescue operation. A cardinal tetra, one of the most popular *piaba* species, would be lucky to live a year in the wild. In a home aquarium, a cardinal might live to two, three, or more.

"This has got to be the world's most benign fishery," Scott explains. The fishers, known locally as *piabeiros* (pee-uh-BEAR-ohs), work from canoes, urging the fish into big handheld nets and then using gourds or buckets to scoop them gently from the water into plastic-lined baskets. And what about other species, scooped up by accident? In many other fisheries—such as in Scott's native New England—unwanted fish, called by-catch, "mostly die on the boat," he says. "But here they're released immediately, exactly where they were living." It's easy for the *piabeiros* to release unwanted fish: in handmade canoes, in contrast with big trawlers, the water is only inches away.

These little fish bring such high prices at the market that the trade in aquarium fish in Barcelos provides sixty percent of the cash income for forty thousand people, most of whom live in a vast jungle of forty-six-thousand square miles. *Piaba* might mean "small fry"—but to be a *piabeiro* is a Big Deal. Think of it: at your local pet store, a cardinal tetra, who weighs only half a gram (.017

Rafael Strella, our Brazilian guide, at the prow of a motorized canoe.

ounces), might cost between four and six dollars. Do the math: There are 1,000 grams in a kilo, and .45 kilos in a pound. Cardinal tetras are worth around $8,000 per kilo, or $3,600 per pound! Sold as treasured pets, these little fish provide far more profits than fish who are captured and killed for people to eat. In fact, pound per pound, these fish are as precious as the rubies and sapphires whose colors they share.

The local people recognize that *piaba* "are the most valuable thing they have," says Scott. "*Piabeiros* and their families protect their river and the forest that surrounds it like their lives depend on it—because they do." In other areas of the Amazon basin, people desperate for jobs might welcome timber barons, cattle ranchers, or mining interests. But here, they're not welcome. *Piabeiros* know that these industries would pollute their waters with silt, dung, or toxic metals. Scott says that after his first visit he

Just outside Manaus, at the Meeting of the Waters, the dark waters of the Río Negro join the light waters of the Río Solimões to form the Amazon River.

understood that the fishery for the aquarium trade "serves as a very effective first line of defense for the rainforest."

"Not only is the fishery not out of control," he adds. "Here we have harmony between humans and the environment in one of the most biologically important places in the world. It's not just a sustainable fishery; it's beneficial. This is paradise saved!"

After returning from that eye-opening expedition, Scott says, he and his colleagues "had the feeling that we'd made a major discovery in the Amazon—not gold, or new tribes," but a different treasure-trove: beautiful small fish who could save the rainforest.

Across the Amazon basin, some four hundred different species of freshwater fish are collected for the aquarium trade. This trade, properly managed, could well provide an "environmentally and socially responsible" alternative to destructive timber extraction, mining, and slash-and-burn agriculture. That's the conclusion of a 2005 convention held in Colombia, organized by the World Wildlife Fund in South America and TRAFFIC, the international wildlife trade monitoring network, and attended by experts from Ecuador, Venezuela, Colombia, Peru, Brazil, and Guyana.

Now we're going to see for ourselves. Scott and his Brazilian counterpart, the economist Mari Balsan, have gathered a group of forty-five people, enough to fill our two big boats, on an expedition up the Río Negro. Some are scientists. Some, like Scott, are professional aquarists. Some sell aquarium fish for a living. Some are fish veterinarians. Some are home hobbyists. Some are students. Some are volunteers. Scott's wife, Tania, who heads the New England

A squirrel monkey—just one of thousands of species that depend on the health of the Amazon's waters and forests.

Aquarium's Sustainable Seafood Programs, is here too, along with their kids, Daniel, four, and Theo, seven. I've come to write this book for you, along with photographer Keith Ellenbogen, who takes the pictures.

We've all come to see the natural, wild environment of some of the fish species that many of us kept in our aquariums as kids. We've come to meet the *piabeiros*. We hope to learn from them how this kind of fishery might help protect other watery environments on continents around the world. We've timed our trip to coincide with a local celebration, the Festival of Ornamental Fish, its songs and dances, floats and fireworks, sure to be a highlight of the journey to Barcelos.

But we've also come to consider some of the problems faced by the *piabeiros* and possibly to help. Even back in 1991 Scott realized that the sustainable fishery here faced some serious issues. Some of the fish collected from the Amazon were arriving at aquariums stressed and sick from their journey. Meanwhile, competing business interests were trying to figure out how to force cardinal tetras and other *piaba* to spawn in captivity and thus be sold cheaply.

That could wipe out the livelihood of the *piabeiros*—forcing them to turn to mining, forest-destroying farming, or even selling drugs.

That's why Scott and his first collaborator, Professor Chao (now retired from the project), founded Project Piaba—to provide the *piabeiros* with support and advice from fish scientists, veterinarians, industry advocates, and policy advisors in order to help both the *piaba* and the *piabeiros* thrive. With the slogan "Buy a fish, save a tree," Project Piaba aims to connect hobbyists and professional aquarists around the world with the people who provide their fish. Together, they can help support the health of the jungle environment that the fish, the *piabeiros*, and more than a thousand other species—including humans—depend on to survive.

Scott comes back to the Amazon year after year, learning new things each time. But this year the expedition has special urgency. Today, he warns, threats to this fishery—some from well-meaning people, others from competing business interests—are more serious than ever. They could not only undermine the local people's livelihoods and culture; they could endanger the Amazon itself.

AMAZON BY THE NUMBERS

Length of Amazon River: 4,000 MILES

Rank of the Amazon among the world's mightiest rivers: 1 (The Nile is longer, but the Amazon carries more water.)

Width of the Amazon as it reaches the sea: 15 MILES

Number of Amazon tributaries: MORE THAN 1,000

Number of these more than 1,000 miles long: 17

Percentage of the South American continent occupied by the Amazon River basin: 40

Number of countries through which the Amazon River flows: 9

Percentage of the world's oxygen contributed by the Amazon rainforest: 20

Percentage of Earth's fresh water discharged from the Amazon: 20

Percentage of the world's animals living in the Amazon rainforest: 10

Species of plants found in the Amazon: 40,000

Species of plants found in the United States: 18,000

Species of fish known from the Amazon River: 5,600

Species of fish in the Mississippi River: 250

Percentage of the modern human diet developed from Amazon plants: UP TO 80

Number of new species discovered in the Amazon since 1999: MORE THAN 1,200

Frequency with which a new species was discovered during a recent Amazon survey: 1 EVERY 3 DAYS

Speed at which the Amazon rainforest is destroyed each year: 2.7 MILLION ACRES

CHAPTER 2
KINGDOM OF THE CARDINALS

"There's a good chance of seeing cardinal tetras today!" Scott tells us. Glowing electric blue and radiant crimson, like the rich robes of high bishops of the Catholic Church for whom they are named, these stunning inch-long beauties are among the most popular aquarium fish in the world. They're found only in the Río Negro and in Venezuela's largest river, the Orinoco.

Since we boarded our boats in Manaus, we've had two beautiful days on the water, happily swapping shoveling January snow for watching a green wall of jungle slide by as pink dolphins surface and toucans shoot like arrows across the river. Some of us have been fishing for piranhas from the top deck. But now, on our third day, we're especially eager to see cardinal tetras swimming free in their wild habitat.

The *Dorinha* has dropped anchor, so we can step gingerly from its lower deck to board motorized canoes for a trip up the Aturia River. It's our first foray into a tribu-tary of the Río Negro. By canoe, it's about an hour to our first stop—an area with shallow

rapids and scoured sinkholes, with water so stained with natural tannins it's as red as burgundy wine. On the way, we stop briefly to watch a single howler monkey running along the thick branch of an ancient fig tree with buttress roots. We spot a sloth near the top of a spindly cecropia tree.

"It's tricky here—we've got to duck!" Scott tells his younger son, Daniel, as our canoe passes beneath the branches of a tree partially submerged in the flooded forest.

In some places the water is so mirror smooth that you cannot tell where the air ends and the water begins. It's easy to see why local people speak of an enchanted world beneath the river, a world that mirrors our own, the way the water mirrors the trees and the sky.

As we watch kingfishers zip across the river and red, gold, and blue parrots alight in the canopies of the trees, beneath our canoe, fish fly like birds between tree branches. It's the wet season, a time of plenty, when abundance overflows like the riverbanks.

Beneath the river's surface, tiny fish shelter in the flooded forest.

Rafael shows the team the fish he has captured.

We pass trees that seem to be barely holding their crowns above water. Life piles upon life: Some trees are encumbered with termite nests bigger than basketballs; others are ornamented like Christmas trees with the purselike, woven-grass nests of orapendulas—big black birds with blue eyes and bright yellow tails. We pass trees that seem to be exploding with orange flower petals and others hung with seedpods that look like round doll heads with crimson crewcuts.

Finally we come to our first stop. It's a shallow area with ruby-colored water. We're hot, eager to enter the cool, dark river. Within a minute, tiny fish are nipping at our skin. We put on our facemasks and lower our bodies into the water to see the fish. We count three different species of tetras. Scott identifies them right away: *Copella,* or splash tetras, are spotted inch-long schooling fish with red and black fins. There's a group of *Bryconops* with red tails and black and yellow fins. Another species is silvery and slender, with a black stripe down each side. Scott identifies this as one of the seventy species of *Characidium* tetras. Many of these live in fast-running water, and some have fins so strong they can grip the rocks at the edges of waterfalls.

But no cardinals. They're shyer than many other tetras; it's no wonder they're more difficult to find. On we go to a second site, this one with waterfalls. In the shallows, sand carried by rushing water has scoured three-foot-deep holes in the rock. Past the falls, Rafael Strella, our Brazilian guide, cuts a short path through the watery forest, leading us to more wonderfully smooth rocks and sandy bottoms. With Scott in the lead, we plunge into the shallows with our masks and snorkels.

We fan out. It's important to move quietly and slowly, and it's best to stay in one place for a while, Scott explains. These tiny fish frighten easily. I stick by Marion Lepzelter, who is thirty-two, a volunteer at the New England Aquarium and with Project Piaba. She's hoping to film many of these Río Negro species in the wild for the project's website, projectpiaba.org.

"Be the driftwood," she advises me, and we both float as still as sticks. Our reward:

from behind some rocks, two flattened disk-shaped fish, their slender faces masked in black and their sides decorated with maze-like patterns of green and fawn, come swimming toward us like rolling coins. Because of their shape, they're known as discus fish; they're found only in the Amazon basin. But as quick as a flash, they disappear. "They may be guarding a nest!" Marion whispers to me as she pulls her head from the water. Discus are cichlids, a large and diverse group of fish related to perch, and soon more cichlids swim into view: Pike cichlids. Pale flag cichlids. Checkerboard cichlids. Marion is thrilled to find them.

But where are the cardinals?

Scott is only a few feet away. He's investigat-ing an area near a wall of smooth rock, where a sandy, leafy hole meets a large tree root.

"I found them!" he cries. "There—down in this hole over here!"

Hiding in eight inches of water, three cardinals are in shadow—but they seem to glow in the dark. "Each fish moves a little differently," explains Scott. Rather than mere swimming, their movement reminds me of the twinkling of stars.

Why do these fish dazzle and shimmer? No one knows for sure. Scott thinks it might help them school. Or they might dazzle their predators just as they dazzle us—and just as we are mesmerized by their magical lights, they turn and, like shooting meteorites, vanish from sight.

The three cardinal tetras disappear before Marion can film them. "They only come out for their king!" Marion says to Scott.

How do you find a handful of inch-long fish in a thousand-mile river?

The next day, we try again. Overnight, we had traveled farther upstream, and we plan to scout a new area. We're hoping to find water where it will be easy to see and film cardinal tetras. But after thirty minutes of motoring our canoe through a maze of drowned trees and draping vines, one thing is clear—and it's not the water.

"We were hoping to find clearer water for photography," says Scott, "but failing that, I'm looking for good habitat." We arrive at an area with gently sloping banks and, growing beneath the water, baby trees with slender trunks and branches that may shelter these shy, tiny fish.

"Watch out for this saw grass," Scott says as we disembark from the canoe. He points to the tall, whiplike blades with serrated edges growing around and in the water. "It will grab you," he warns his kids. "It's like barbed wire, and it'll hurt."

Scott slips into the water as gently and easily as a person falling asleep on a hot day. Wearing stubby fins and his snorkel and

A striped headstander.

mask, the big man becomes weightless in the water's embrace. He not so much swims like a fish in the water as he floats like a cloud in the sky, gently, patiently, waiting for the *piaba* to come.

While Marion and I are still taking off our shoes, Scott has gone to work. "He's already finding fish!" Marion says. "Yup, he's the fish finder!" echoes four-year-old Daniel. While Theo heads to a different spot with his mom, Daniel climbs on his dad's back as if he were riding a dolphin.

Less than a minute passes before Scott pulls his face from the water. *"Crenicichla regani!"* he announces, speaking the species' Latin name. Then, for my benefit, he uses the common name, the name you'd find posted by its tank in a pet store: checkerboard cichlid. It's a beautiful black and silver checked fish that's called *xadrez shah drayz* in Brazilian Portuguese—"the chessboard."

"Cichlids are related to sunfish and bass," he explains. "And a lot of times, dwarf cichlids are found with cardinal tetras."

Scott has found productive hunting grounds. "There are cool little fish of many species here everywhere!" he says.

Marion joins him in the shallow water. Within minutes, she spots a gorgeous tiny fish with a pink neon stripe, a species she doesn't recognize. "It's like a pencil fish without the black," she says. "It could be a new species! Do you think," she asks Scott, "that we could be seeing fish that are undescribed by science?"

"Yes," answers Scott firmly.

Scott swims in the Amazon, looking for tropical fish.

ABOVE: A checkerboard cichlid. BELOW: A juvenile dwarf pike.   ABOVE: A pristella tetra. BELOW: A Cupid cichlid.

Scott's four-year-old son, Daniel, rides his dad's back as the two explore the river for fish.

"And what would you call a plain silver tetra?" asks Marion.

"Anything you want," answers Scott. Like the pencil fish with the pink stripe, it could be a new species too. Scientists estimate that only one-quarter of the plants and animals on Earth have been identified. Hundreds, if not thousands, of the fish in the Amazon may remain as yet undescribed by scientists, undiscovered by anyone but the people and other animals who live here.

"Well, there's one right now under the checkerboard cichlid," says Marion.

Scott has swum ahead about fifty yards. The water's surface is only two to three feet above the soft, leaf-littered bottom. But because of sticks, saw grass, and stingrays (they often hide buried in the bottom, and a sting from the poison-tipped spines on their tails can hurt for days) as well as the possibility of sudden drop-offs, it's smarter to swim than to walk. Plus there's less chance of kicking up dirt to cloud the water.

"Let's see . . ." Scott mumbles through his snorkel—a "language" we call Snorkelese that sounds like it's spoken through the nose. "Right at first glance, a lot of really good species are just coming out!"

But I am frustrated. I can see none of them—until Scott shows me how.

There's a technique for making "invisible" little fish suddenly appear. "Look for good habitat," Scott tells me. "They like trees and cover. It's not really looking for fish; it's looking for habitat.

"At first, you scare them off," he continues. "If you chase them, they'll swim away. But if you stay still, they get curious. Stop and wait. Get in fairly deep, in a place where you're comfortable, and just stay still and watch. The fish," he promises, "will come to you."

We float among the submerged tree branches, our faces in the water, our ears above. We hear the whistles and burbles of birds, sounds as liquid and cool as the dark water. From previous trips to the Amazon, I recognize the rattling call of the kingfisher; the high, ascending song of the green-tailed jacamar, which increases in tempo like a Ping-Pong ball trapped under a paddle; the screams of a pair of parrots. They are surely discussing their errands as they wing just inches from each other through a sky silvery with coming rain.

And in a minute I see that Scott was right: like magic, little fish appear. Silvery scales flash. Gossamer fins flutter. Some come close enough to nibble gently on my hands.

"I've got a couple of checkerboards and some other tetras over here," calls Marion. "And there are definitely actual pencil fish over here. A whole school of them just swam by me . . ."

"Some of these fish have red fins, and some of them have black spots on the fins!" another snorkeler calls to Scott.

The red of the fins doesn't register with Scott. He is red-green colorblind. For most of us, color is the main way we identify fish, as well as birds and many other animals. But Scott knows fish so well he doesn't need color. He identifies them by their pattern and shape and by the unique way each species moves.

We've been in for only half an hour and already Scott has spotted several dozen species, some he doesn't recognize. "Watch for the yellowish fins of *Biotodoma cupido*," he spouts in Snorkelese. This fish is also known as the Cupid cichlid, and Scott doesn't want us to miss it, as the species is such a beauty—a deep-bodied fish with lemon yellow fins and a black dot surrounded with yellow on each of its sides.

Many of these fish are as interesting in their habits as they are striking in appearance. For instance, the one spot eartheater grabs a mouthful of dirt and silt, sifts it for nutrients, then spits the rest out through its gills. The spotted headstander has an upturned mouth, and while it's turned upside down, it feeds on slimy bacteria that adhere to the surface of plants. The marbled hatch-

etfish—the one that flies out of the water to escape predators—has its mouth on top of its head! Why? Because food often falls into the water from above.

Other species we're seeing here are dwarf cichlids—called *Apistogramma gibbiceps*—small, with blue scales and a spade-shaped tail, and *Satanoperca lilith,* with reddish fins, a black spot, and golden eyes. "I have some of those behind my desk at the aquarium," Scott says. And many others are on display for the public in his Amazon tank.

"When I see this," he says, "I think, How can I make my exhibits at the New England Aquarium look more like this?"

Not many people get to see these beautiful fish in the wild as we're doing. But if these creatures are to survive in the wild, it's essential that people around the world care about protecting them. That's part of what Scott's doing here, too.

"I'm making this a goal," he announces. "For people standing in a cement building on Boston Harbor—even if it's snowing out to be able to see *this*."

Theo, seven, enjoys an encounter with a pink dolphin who has learned to expect fish from an Amazon family. Theo is Scott and Tania's older son.

17

MEETING THE SEVEN DEADLY PLAGUES OF THE AMAZON—IN THE DARK!

Keith wants photos of fish swimming through the branches of the underwater trees. One morning, we persuade our guide, Rafael, to take Keith, me, and fellow Project Piaba travelers Dan Rabb and Jason Spiro via motorized canoe to an area Keith calls the Valley of the Drowned Trees. The water here is very dark. Rafael ties our canoe to one of the saplings, near what we think might be shallows. But how deep is the water? We can't see. We poke Dan's GoPro pole in; it's only five feet long and doesn't touch bottom. Where *is* the bottom? And more important, *who* is on the bottom?

Keith doesn't want to step on a STINGRAY. These flattened relatives of sharks hide buried in mud and sand. If disturbed, a stingray might strike out with its tail, inflicting pain from its venomous tip that burns for days. (One of these actually killed the TV star and conservationist Steve Irwin when the barb freakishly penetrated his heart.) It's just one of the animals visitors have dubbed the Seven Deadly Plagues of the Amazon. As Keith readies his photo gear, Rafael takes a moment to introduce to us the stories associated with the six other plagues:

• The giant catfish called JAO (pronounced "Jow—OOH") is known as the Monster of the Amazon. Growing to more than three hundred pounds, it is big enough to swallow you whole—but prefers to drag you down to the depths to drown you.

• The ELECTRIC EEL can generate more than six hundred volts—five times the power of a U.S. wall socket. That's strong enough to knock a horse off its feet—and easily enough to kill a human.

• The ANACONDA, the largest and heaviest snake in the world, can grow to more than three hundred pounds. Wrapping twenty feet of muscular coils around its prey and squeezing it to death, this giant snake can eat anything it wants, including jaguars—and people.

• The BLACK CAIMAN, the largest predator in the Amazon basin, is the biggest member of the alligator family, growing to twenty feet. Lurking in the shallows of slow-moving rivers, it may seize prey as big as a tapir (an animal that looks like a cross between a hippo, a pig, and an elephant). Humans make easy prey.

• The PIRANHA hunts in packs, the way wolves do. After President Theodore Roosevelt visited the Amazon in 1913, he famously wrote that schools of these razor-toothed fish are capable of feeding frenzies that can strip a cow to a skeleton in seconds.

• The CANDIRU is probably the scariest of them all. There are several species, but the smallest ones pack the biggest punch. The locals say that if you pee in the water, a candiru will follow the urine to its source—right up inside you—where (yes, it gets worse) it erects spines to hold it in place while it feasts on your flesh. The only way to remove it is by surgery.

Rafael assures us that all Seven Deadly Plagues can be found here in the water. Then Keith goes overboard.

One of the many species of candiru catfish—perhaps the most feared of the so-called Seven Deadly Plagues.

Keith took this self-portrait in the
dark waters of the Río Negro.

"This is so strange!" he exclaims. "Twigs are bumping against my legs. It's weird. You can't tell if what's touching you is a rock or a stingray or a caiman. The things I do for you, Sy!"

Keith submerges completely. We wait in the boat; he doesn't want the rest of us to go in lest we stir up the bottom and cloud the pictures.

Keith spouts through his snorkel. His breathing reminds us of the Creature from the Black Lagoon. Certainly our current location, with its dark, mysterious waters full of unseen lives, recalls the setting for the famous horror movie.

"You know what's totally amazing?" he says, surfacing and withdrawing his snorkel from his mouth. "There's a light wall. The first six inches or so are light, relative to the rest of the water. But I can barely see my hands, and I can't see my feet at all."

Keith dives again. We see him testing his camera's flash; it looks like an underwater lightning storm. He spouts as he surfaces and tells us, "Your legs are bumping against a lot of things—all of which feel like something death-defying! But I don't understand why I'm not seeing fish."

Above us, a green-and-rufous kingfisher chatters. He's looking for fish too.

Though Keith has seen no fish, his experience is still thrilling. He's exploring an underwater forest, a world like ours yet not like ours, familiar and strange at once. In our northern forests we might see lichens growing on trees; here you might see freshwater sponges growing on them. And though we're used to birds flying through branches in our forests, birds show up in flooded forests, too—as Keith discovers.

BAM! Right in front of him, the king-fisher slams into the water like a lawn dart!

"*%$&!" Keith spouts, surfacing in alarm. "What was *that*?" An electric eel? An ana-conda?

The flooded forest is different from any habitat Keith has explored in more than a quarter century of scuba diving, snorkeling, and photographing in the sea. "In the ocean, there's a big fish that might bite you"—but at least you can see it. "It's helpful to anticipate what might take you down."

He submerges again, this time in shal-lower water. And finally the fish appear. We can see some of them from the canoe, revealed by a single ray of sunlight striking the water. "It's amazing how it looks at first like nothing is there," says Dan, "and then, suddenly, you see them all!"

To our left, in deeper water, Rafael spots a peacock bass. "He's hunting the other fish," he tells us—which is surely why all the fish were hiding earlier.

Beneath the water, Keith moves forward slowly through the dark, holding his big camera in his two hands in front of his face as he kicks with his fins, careful not to stir up the bottom and cloud the water. Finally he is in water shallow enough to stand, and he bends at a 90-degree angle, like an open book, in order to steady his camera for a macro shot. And then—

"*Pffthth!*" Startled, Keith shoots the water from his snorkel and surfaces in a hurry. "There was a catfish right under my fin!" Was it the dreaded jao?

Keith ducks back beneath the water and holds still. And now the small fish come. In the red-tinted murk he can see inch-long fish with spotted fins, others with black stripes, still more with upturned mouths. They are all around him now—but, alas, not close enough for his macro lens. He surfaces to report: "The fish here are little, they're camouflaged, they're subtle. This is as pretty a place as you can imagine, though," he says.

Rafael tells us it's time to get back to the *Dorinha*. Reluctantly, Keith swims over to the canoe. As he fins toward us, we notice that he has an entourage. Dozens of little fish trail in his wake, like the tail on a comet. Is this some kind of fishy joke? "Great," says Keith. "They're all following me now."

At the New England Aquarium, Scott's Amazon tank showcases species he found in the wild.

CHAPTER 3
SCOTT'S STORY

"Sea monkeys!"

According to Scott's family lore, these were the first two words he uttered as an infant.

Back onboard the top deck of the *Dorinha,* as we steam toward Barcelos under sunny skies, Scott tells me how tending fish has always played a pivotal role in his life.

He was the youngest of six kids, and his playpen was in a room where one of his siblings had set up an aquarium for Sea-Monkeys—the brand name for brine shrimp sold in popular hatching kits. When little Scott noticed the tiny babies hatching out, he started screaming his head off: *"Sea monkeys! Sea monkeys!"*

Scott tends to the Amazon tank from behind the scenes.

By the time he was old enough for kindergarten, Scott was often off with his brothers and sister, catching sunfish and tadpoles, exploring Cranberry Pond near his home in Weymouth, Massachusetts. They brought the tadpoles home to watch them turn into frogs, and soon Scott had amassed quite a menagerie: fish, frogs, salamanders, turtles. He also rescued birds with broken wings. "My mom had only one rule: no snakes," he remembers. But he couldn't resist taking home a snake, too. "My mom only found out about the snake because me and my siblings were looking under the furniture for it." (It was a harmless garter snake.)

By the time Scott was seven, the creatures he brought home from Cranberry Pond had more company. Housing them in tanks scavenged from neighbors' trash and bought from yard sales, he now kept pet cardinals, splash tetras, and swordtails, bought with money earned from doing yard work around the neighborhood, and later, a paper route. He loved to ride his Schwinn Stingray downtown to his favorite pet store, Barks N' Bubbles, to watch the fish there.

"Rowdy kids would come and slam on the tanks," Scott remembers. "The owner, Joe, would breathe fire on these kids. And he'd say to me, 'Can you believe those kids?'"

The pet-store owner knew that Scott was different. He wasn't a bother. He let Joe work. He didn't touch stuff. Most of the time in the pet store he acted as if he were invisible. He watched; he listened—just as one day in the Amazon he would float, still and silent, waiting for tiny wild fish to come out from hiding.

Joe changed water in the tanks all day long, siphoning out old water and refilling with fresh. One day, Scott remembers, Joe left the water running in a tank while he was talking with customers. Scott saw that the tank was about to overflow. It was then, he says, that he flew into action: "I broke from my invisibility cloak and crossed the line." He moved the hose just in time. "And over the customer's shoulder," he recalls, "Joe gave me a little nod. *That's* when I became an aquarist."

When Scott got older, around age twelve, he'd ride his bike farther from home. He'd cycle to Quincy, duck under the turnstiles to the subway, and get out at the aquarium stop in Boston. His parents had taken him, as a baby in diapers, to the aquarium on its opening day, June 20, 1969, and he'd been

Scott communes with one of the two electric eels.

enchanted ever since. He'd sneak into the aquarium by putting a smudge on his hand that looked like the entry stamp for paying patrons, and he'd spend the day watching fish to his heart's content.

By the time he was a teenager, Scott had several dozen tanks at home. "I'd hang out in the basement with my fish and wonder about my future," he remembers. He was distressed that his siblings seemed to have already chosen their career paths, fulfilling their destinies. A brother had played with a pedal police car as a tot; now he was preparing for a career in law enforcement. His

sister, who had loved to dress up as a nurse, was in college, studying nursing. "And I'd come up from the basement . . . everyone else knew their thing, and I'm just playing with fish." By the end of high school Scott figured that he might as well become an accountant like his dad—though he didn't think he'd like it.

Then one day he was watching George Page in *Nature* on TV "and a light bulb went off in my head." He thought, "I *do* have a thing! This is what I'm all about!" Within weeks of that realization he became a volunteer at the aquarium. He was eighteen.

As two pink dolphins rise, gasp, and dive back beneath the dark river, Scott remembers his first day at the New England Aquarium. "They told me the job wouldn't be glamorous. It was wet, smelly work, chopping fish and cleaning floors." But immediately he was set up with a wetsuit, and his first task was helping draw blood from an Atlantic white-sided dolphin!

At ten A.M. on his first day of volunteering Scott found himself kneeling in a tank in which the water level had been lowered to two feet, working with a team of experts, wrestling with a dolphin named Silver, a stranding victim who was sick with a respiratory disease. Scott couldn't believe his luck.

As everyone held the dolphin still, the aquarium's top dolphin specialist told the team, "Whatever you do, nobody put your face over the blowhole!" Silver's respiratory disease could have been contagious; it was possible that humans could catch it. "But with all the adrenaline pumping and the white noise," Scott remembers, "what I heard was 'Somebody—put your face over the blowhole!' But nobody was doing it! And I was the only one in the face-over-the-blowhole position." So he immediately stuck his face right over the diseased dolphin's blowhole.

His boss yanked Scott up by the hair.

Days later, poor Silver died of his respiratory infection. But Scott remained healthy. And despite his early mistake, he thrived as a volunteer.

Still, he wasn't doing so great at school. "I started going to UMass Boston, and I did terrible," he admits. "I had a GPA of .86. I wasn't much of a reader. I'm not a book person, and college involves a lot of books." He was learning much more at the aquarium than at school, and he found himself volunteering more and more hours—sometimes instead of going to classes.

Then he had another stroke of luck— and he was in the right place at the right time to benefit. He had been volunteering for a year and a half when the head of the Fishes Department called Scott into his office. It was a busy time at the aquarium: there had been a mass pilot whale stranding on Cape Cod, and the staff had rescued three of them for rehabilitation and release. An aquarist had left, and a job opening needed to be filled—fast. Would Scott take the job?

You bet he would!

By age twenty-one Scott found himself taking charge not only of the aquarium's popular tide pool exhibit but also of the institution's newest changing exhibit—an Amazon-themed gallery, complete with rainforest canopy, hummingbirds, emerald tree boas, poison arrow frogs, walking stick insects, and tanks of Amazonian fish, including cardinal tetras.

Soon after his first trip to South America, he would be able to concentrate exclusively on his specialty—freshwater animals. Though he never completed his undergraduate degree, he would go on to earn a master's degree in aquaculture from the University of Stirling in Scotland. He wrote his thesis on how to reduce stress in cardinal tetras exported from the Río Negro to aquariums in Scotland.

This was an ambitious project. How can you tell if a tiny fish is feeling stress? But it was an important question. You can't always tell that a fish is stressed by looking at it. Yet stress can kill a fish, weakening its immune system enough that it can succumb to infections, parasites, and injuries that otherwise would pose no danger. But how do you measure stress response in the blood chemistry of a fish so small?

Scott adapted such gadgets as glucose meters used by diabetics for use in the field on these tiny animals. He tested the blood for a hormone called cortisol, the same hormone associated with stress in human beings. He discovered that tiny cardinal tetras could, in fact, be subjected to dangerous stresses during their long trip. And he found that not all fish were suffering. What made the difference?

Thanks to this new set of instruments and the data they made possible, Scott could next focus on subtle differences in the way individual fishers handled the animals. He found, for instance, that there was a huge difference between fish scooped up with kitchen strainers and ones collected in hollow gourds. The kitchen strainers damaged the protective mucus coating of the fish and hurt their delicate skin.

Scott began the series of studies that many onboard the *Dorinha* and its sister ship, the *Iracema,* will continue to expand upon on this trip. What "best handling practices" can be developed to protect the fish from stress and disease, make them competitive in the global market, and return the most benefits to the fishing communities that are the stewards of the environment?

Keeping fish healthy and happy is a job Scott deals with every day at the New England Aquarium. In Boston, he is in charge of two electric eels, one three-foot-long and three thirteen-foot-long anacondas, fifteen red-bellied piranhas, 2,644 cardinal tetras, and ten thousand other freshwater animals—from fish to turtles to toads—all of them in leafy, naturalistic exhibits that he

Scott works with volunteer April Pinnick to prune plants in the electric eel exhibit.

is constantly improving. He wants to keep his animals in peak condition. He loves each one. And equally important, each creature in his Amazon gallery is an ambassador for its jungle home.

Scott hopes to bring visitors "face to face with the Amazon" when they look in on one of these tanks—even in sometimes snowy Boston. It's an experience he considers essential. "More than a million people come through the New England Aquarium in a year," he says, "and we need to change the lives of *all* of them. We need to turn them into conservationists."

On the *Dorinha,* it's now five p.m., and two macaws fly overhead. They disappear into the leafy crown of a huge buttressed tree on the riverbank. "This time of day, you see a lot of parrots," Scott explains. Because we're so near the equator, the sun sets around six every night, year-round, and rises around six each morning. The parrots are finding safe roosts where they can spend the night.

Soon we'll be heading for bed too. After dinner we'll retreat to our cabin bunks early. Tomorrow we'll arrive in Barcelos—where we'll join the throngs getting ready for the Ornamental Fish Festival, the biggest celebration of the year.

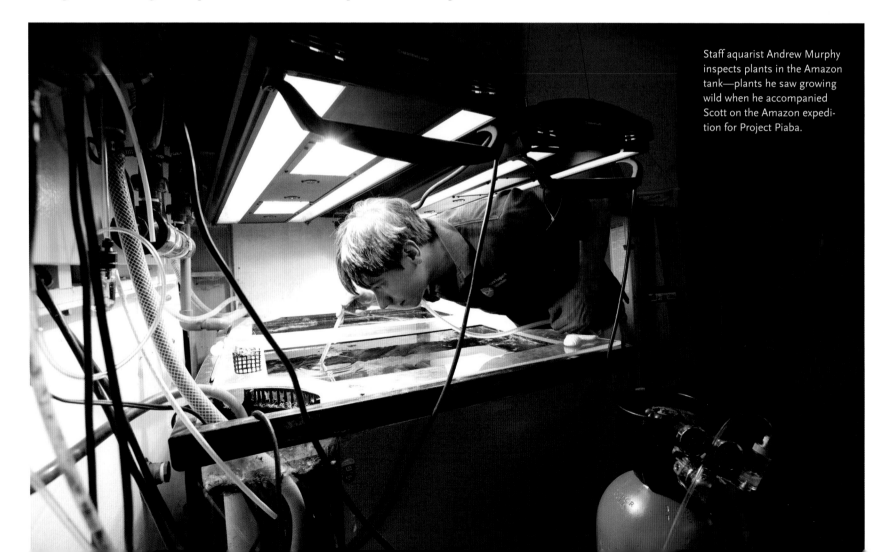

Staff aquarist Andrew Murphy inspects plants in the Amazon tank—plants he saw growing wild when he accompanied Scott on the Amazon expedition for Project Piaba.

THE SEVEN DEADLY PLAGUES OF THE AMAZON DEBUNKED (SORT OF)

- **STINGRAY:** The poison-tipped tail spine is no joke. The fish deploys this defensive weapon the way a scorpion wields a stinger, whipping it forward in a fraction of a second. Strong and sharp enough to penetrate bone, the spine breaks off in the wound. The stingray can grow a new spine—but leaves its victim with an unhappy problem, because the spine is barbed like an arrowhead, and very difficult to extract. But extract it you must, because until you do, the poisonous mucus with which it's covered will continue to dissolve your flesh. The good news is that stingrays don't attack. They use the tail spine only in self-defense. And happily, there's a sure-fire way to avoid them. Scott showed us how to do the Stingray Shuffle: When you walk along the bottom, slide your feet along instead of stepping. The stingrays will graciously move out of the way.

- **JAO:** They do get very large—big enough that it would take three or four strong men to hold one up out of the water. But you are more likely to eat a jao catfish than a jao is likely to eat you. On the Internet you can see lots of photos of fishermen proudly holding up giant jao catfish. What you won't see is any real evidence that one ever killed a person. How did the jao get such a bad rep? When you travel everywhere on the water, drowning is a serious danger (like a car crash for people who travel on roads), and many catfish scavenge any corpses they can find, including those of humans.

- **ELECTRIC EEL:** Yes, it can give you a painful shock—but only if you bother it. Electric eels, who are more closely related to carp and catfish than to the freshwater eels we know from North America and Europe, are amazingly common in Amazon waters (one survey found they were the most abundant fish in the stretch of river studied!), but they seldom bother people. To find their prey and navigate with their weak eyes in the flooded forest, they emit a low-level charge, less than ten volts, which doesn't hurt. Electric eels save their powerful blasts for stunning prey and repelling predators.

- **ANACONDA:** These big snakes certainly *could* eat people—but they don't. In 2014, as a TV stunt, a filmmaker wearing a custom-built snake-proof suit *tried* to get eaten by an anaconda—and failed. The world's top expert on anacondas, Jesus Rivas, knows of no documented instance of an anaconda eating a human, ever—though he admits that most people purposely stay away from areas where they know these giant snakes live.

- **BLACK CAIMAN:** Growing to six hundred pounds, living for nearly a century, this largest of the six species of South American caimans is so strong that only a jaguar can kill an adult (and the jaguar doesn't always win). But the

A stingray, with its poisonous spine,
lies mostly hidden under the sand.

caiman's worst predators are humans. In the 1950s and '60s, people killed so many black caimans for their meat and skins that the species nearly went extinct. Happily, they are now making a comeback. The Brazilian conservation biologist Ronis Da Silveira has captured and tagged more than three thousand of them—including a fifteen-footer he wrestled for forty minutes—and he insists that if you don't bother them, they are rather calm.

• PIRANHA: "Aren't piranhas dangerous?" This is one of the most frequent questions Scott is asked. "The standard answer," he says, "is 'only when they're spawning.'" But there was a time when he and a colleague were snorkeling in shallow water in the middle of an intense piranha spawning frenzy. Piranhas were bouncing off their heads, but they were never bitten—nor was Scott when, as an experiment, he offered one of the supposedly most "aggressive" species of piranha his bleeding hand. What about Theodore Roosevelt's stories? Turns out that the local people, eager to impress a visiting American president, held a bunch of piranhas captive for days without feeding them—and then released them, allowing the president to watch them feed hungrily on chunks of horse meat.

• CANDIRU: What this tiny fish is reputed to do sure makes it one of the scariest of the Seven Deadly Plagues. The researcher Stephen Spotte spent four years investigating the stories, traveling the Amazon, talking with locals, fish researchers, and doctors, and he could not find a single scientifically documented case of this happening. Only in 1997 did researchers discover a single—and so far the only—documented case: an unfortunate twenty-three-year-old man who was urinating in knee-deep water. Here are the facts: There are a number of species of candiru, some up to sixteen inches long, others tiny. All of them are catfish and have specialized to become parasites. They usually lodge in other fishes' gill openings and feed on their blood. They will also infest human corpses, and body openings (as vultures know well) are always a good point of entry—which might be the way the stories started.

CHAPTER 4
BARCELOS

On Saturday morning, the day we arrive, the riverbank is already lined with boats: three-tiered riverboats with such intriguing names as *Amazonas de Deus, Tayacu 2, Cala Luna,* and *Baragatu.* A huge ferry is hung with hammocks, like bunting. Dozens of smaller houseboats, handmade from wood, with tin roofs, crowd the shallows.

Only twenty-five thousand people live in Barcelos (Boston has almost thirty times that number of people). But the Festival of Ornamental Fish briefly doubles the town's population. Twenty thousand more people come from as far away as the nation's capital, Brasília, to join the famous celebration of the little fish who are the lifeblood of the town.

Here in Barcelos, we on the *Dorinha* are happy to have joined up with our sister ship, the *Iracema,* and the fish biologists, students, friends, and aquarium specialists onboard—especially bubbly, warm Mari Balsan, Scott's Brazilian partner in Project Piaba. She has been working with the project since earning her master's degree in 2009, and even

though she's originally from the south of Brazil, she says that Barcelos and the villages of the region now "feel like home" to her.

We newcomers are eager to explore this pretty town, with its cement buildings painted in lavender and lime—or red and blue like the cardinals—its streets lined with palms, and its gardens fragrant with bougainvillea blossoms. We want to get a look at the Piabodrome, the stadium where the action will take place this evening, and where the competing teams of performers are finishing their floats.

First, though, we have an important meeting with the very people whose work we will celebrate at the festival tonight: the fishers who collect the *piaba* for export.

That morning, at a riverside restaurant beneath a woven bamboo ceiling, we meet with twenty-five fishers—one of whom is a seventy-seven-year-old grandmother—who are members of the ornamental fish cooperative, Ornapesca. Mari addresses the group:

"At first they were known as the *Gringos Doidos*—the crazy white foreigners," she tells

Almost every home in Barcelos is preparing for the Festival of Ornamental Fish, the biggest event of the year.

O POVO TEM CONFIANCA, CARDINAL E A ESPERANCA E A RIQUEZA DO LUGAR.

LINDO É TE OLHAR NAS AGUAS MANEIRAS CARDINAL BRILHAR

"You have a very large variety of beautiful fish," he says as Mari translates to Portuguese. "For us in the industry, it's important to see fish from all over the world, but now there are captive-bred, pond-raised fish in other countries competing with your fish. The cardinal tetras from the Río Negro are more beautiful," Gerald explains, "but they sometimes arrive in poor condition because of the long distances they have to travel."

That's where Scott's and Mari's boatloads of fish experts come in: they're here to help the fishers—as well as the people at the transfer stations where fish are held before traveling to home aquariums around the world—make sure that the wild Río Negro fish are captured, held, and transported under the most comfortable, healthy conditions possible so they arrive at their new homes in better condition than the ones artificially farmed in Asian and North American ponds.

Because their fishery protects wild habitat, the fish from the pristine waters of the Río Negro are more valuable than captive-raised ones—but many hobbyists may not know this. But now, Mari tells the fishers, Project Piaba has found a new way to get that message across. Thanks to three years of intensive effort, she has secured a huge international honor for these little locals: A world body of experts has officially awarded Río Negro tetras "geographical indication"

the group in Brazilian Portuguese. When Scott and his friends first showed up in Brazil in 1991, few of the locals could figure out why people had come from so far away just to see the little fish who lived in their rivers, and they concluded that the gringos must be *doido*—crazy! "But this group of aquarists from foreign lands—researchers, importers, veterinarians—represents a great resource and great opportunities for partnering with the fishing community," Mari says.

"The market is huge for the fish out of here," she says as Scott translates to English for us gringos, "and the fishery is abundant. We just have to fix some of the links that are broken."

João de Souza Freitas, president of the cooperative, knows too well that his livelihood is threatened. In the year 2000, he says, a thousand households in Barcelos were employed as *piabeiros*. Today there are still plenty of fish, but only three hundred people make their living fishing for them. They used to get orders for ten thousand cardinals in a week. Today they might get orders for a few hundred a week.

What happened? Gerald Bassleer, a dapper Belgian wearing glasses and a goatee, joined Scott's team on the *Iracema* to come to Barcelos and explain. He's a specialist in fish diseases and the president of the worldwide trade group Ornamental Fish International.

(GI) status. It's a name or sign famously used on foods, such as French champagne or English Cheddar cheese, to identify these items as the most authentic version of the product, owing to the special places they come from. Río Negro cardinal tetras are the first live animals to be so honored.

Project Piaba also wants to assure buyers of wild fish that the animals were handled with the most skilled, caring, humane techniques, Mari explains to the *piabeiros*. So Project Piaba's scientists and veterinarians will be working with Brazilian students to share what they've discovered in their research: the best ways to keep the fish calm, comfortable, and healthy on their long journey from the Río Negro to people's home aquariums.

Gerald from Ornamental Fish International is excited about the geographical indication status—a special seal of quality displayed on pet-store fish tanks and promoted throughout the industry—which should help the Río Negro wild fish command top dollar. "I'm happy this kind of project is giving a new future for the industry and the hobby," Gerald tells the fishers at the meeting. "We need your fish!"

João Freitas, the Ornapesca president, is thrilled. He's been working as a *piabeiro* for thirty of his forty-three years, he says. "I have waited a long time for this," he tells

us through Mari. "It's so important to have Project Piaba's support!"

As we explore the town of Barcelos, it's easy to see why the fishers are glad to receive help in order to keep their sustainable fishery going. Just a glance around town reveals the two things held most dear in the people's hearts: God and fish.

The low skyline is dominated by a pretty blue and white Catholic church. The other most prominent building, the Hotel Río Negro, sports a lively mural of parrots, fishermen, cardinal tetras, discus, and hatchetfish. Along the riverfront, on the town's main street, a cement statue of a peacock bass stands six feet high and stretches thirteen feet long. Not far away, another cement statue shows Jesus standing on a pedestal that is decorated with cardinal tetras. Jesus is holding his hands out wide—as if, locals joke, he is bragging about the size of his catch.

With fish playing such a central role in people's lives, it's no wonder that more than twenty years earlier, in 1994, the townspeople decided to hold the first Ornamental Fish Festival. "It's not enough just to celebrate the fish," Scott had explained to us. "They actually *compete* at who can celebrate the fish the best!"

The festival showcases the efforts of two competing teams: the Cardinal (*Cardinal*) and the Discus (*Disco*). Each team works for months to mount its own two-hour-plus extravaganza, with floats, lights, fireworks, costumes, songs, poetry, and dancing that lasts deep into the night. Each year, the same characters appear: the Cardinal and Discus queens; the Indian tribes, including a shaman; the native Flora and Fauna; the *piabeiros;* and of course the respective fish. But each year they are combined in new ways, with new themes and new costumes, floats, songs, and dances.

A statue of Jesus with hands held out wide. The local fishers here joke that Jesus is saying "I caught a fish THIS big!"

A member of the Cardinal team getting dressed in her costume.

Beto Lima at his upstairs workshop in Barcelos. He came from 560 miles away to work on costumes for the festival.

The winning team is judged not only on the quality and originality of the performance but also on how its supporters behave. Judges rate the fans in the Piabodrome stands not only for how enthusiastically they cheer their own team but also for how politely they watch their rivals. Booing is unheard of; leaving the Piabodome during the other team's performance is penalized.

That's because, though members of rival teams are friends and neighbors, allegiances run deep. "I grew up Cardinal," Saanna Lacerda Cram tells us. Her mother, she explains, is the president of the Cardinal team. Her house is painted red and blue to prove it. A red and blue flag flies year-round in the front yard. Across the street,

neighbors sport a yellow and black Discus flag—"so my aunt went out and bought a bigger Cardinal flag—and flew it higher than my neighbors!"

Saanna came all the way from Boston to be at the festival this year. She's returning to the town where she was born, where her uncle still works as a *piabeiro*. She's been dancing in the festival ever since the first one, when she was fourteen, and she danced every year—until she married an American and moved to Boston. He was a fish hobbyist who came along with Scott on one of Scott's annual trips in 2004! Saanna speaks perfect English, and she generously offers to show us around town as the people are busily getting ready for the Big Night. It

seems that every home and every business in town is involved.

Next door to Saanna's mom, her aunt Mariana and four friends are sewing the last sequins on the eyes of the cutout cardinal tetras that decorate the flags that fans wave in the stands to show their support. At the beauty parlor, fans are getting their nails done—in red and blue for Cardinals, in yellow and black for the Discus team. All up and down the streets, homes are littered with feathered headdresses and sequins as families pitch in to sew flags or finish costumes.

Across the street from the Hotel Macedo, Beto Lima is at work on Indian headdresses. He lives in Caracaraí, 560 miles from here and 370 miles from Manaus,

Mermaid and waterfall floats under construction.

The tucanaré float, shaped like a giant fish, will have moving parts.

but for the past month he's been laboring in his rented workshop up three flights of stairs. He's a professional costume maker, and he came to Barcelos a month ago to make some of the more elaborate costumes for the Cardinal team. Feathers, flowers, beads, fake fur, braided palm leaves, and plastic tusks litter the floor. He will also play the role of a shaman in the performance for the Cardinal team.

We make our way toward the three-thousand-seat Piabodrome, the open-air cement stadium where the festival will take place. Folks are very serious about their teams, Saanna explains as we walk. "They don't want anybody talking bad about their fish." But sometimes there are different allegiances within a family. On our way, Saanna introduces us to Leila Belem, a choreographer with the Discus team. She's one of five professional dancers who design and teach the movements to the team's more than one hundred dancers, who range in age from four to about fifty. Yet, whispers Saanna, "her sister is a Cardinal. *Different fish!*" she exclaims in amazement.

At the Piabodrome, shirtless men are sweating in the heat as they weld the light metal rods ordinarily used in cement sidewalks to complete the skeletons for floats. Others, further along in their work, are applying coats of spray paint. One float is going to be a giant mermaid; another is a copy of the blue and white church; others look as if they are going to be entire landscapes, with opening doors, lights, trees, and flowers. Several floats are still taking shape and, like the skeletons of dinosaurs in a natural history museum, still leave much to the imagination. "The Discus team's floats," observes Saanna with a frown, "are big. Really big. It makes me worried!"

Not much point in worrying now, we tell her. Only five hours remain for the workers to finish the floats, for the dancers to don their costumes, for the artists to apply the performers' makeup, and for all to get ready for the carefully choreographed extravaganza the town has been preparing for all year.

The festival begins at nine p.m. The countdown has begun.

BY DEFENDING THE RIVER, THE *PIABEIROS* ALSO PROTECT . . . THE DOLPHIN WITH MAGICAL POWERS

It looks like a dolphin—but when you get a really good look, it's clearly like no dolphin you've ever seen in the ocean or in an aquarium. The long beak sticks out like a nose. The forehead is humped. The flippers are huge, almost like wings. And the skin is sometimes gray, sometimes whitish—and sometimes dazzlingly, impossibly pink!

So much about these dolphins seems impossible. These creatures live not in the ocean, but in rivers—only in the Amazon and its tributaries, and the Orinoco. They don't leap high, like marine dolphins. Instead, they swing their flexible necks to and fro as they swim through the submerged branches of the flooded forest.

The local people say they are magic. They call them *Encantados* (en-con-TOD-ohs)—"the enchanted ones"—and say that they can transform into people, get out of the water, and dance! They say the dolphin people are

so talented and beautiful, you will fall in love if you meet them. But be careful: Local legend has it that the *Encantados* entice people away from land to the *Encante*, the enchanted world beneath the river. And if you go, you may never return—because everything is more beautiful there.

The dolphins' magic used to protect them. For many years, most native people wouldn't harm them, because they believed in the dolphins' powers. Some said that a dolphin could shoot poison darts out of its blowhole if it got mad! But today, though there's not enough data on their population numbers to classify them as endangered, they are threatened by big commercial food-fishing, by pollution from runoff from logging and cattle operations, and by foreigners who kill these intelligent dolphins and cut them up to use as bait for catfish.

With exquisite sonar, a flexible neck, and front flippers like wings, the pink river dolphin can fly like a bird through the drowned branches of flooded trees in the Río Negro's dark waters.

Cardinal team queen Suellen Paraiso, being dressed by her attendants.

CHAPTER 5
FESTIVAL OF THE FISH

Suellen Paraiso, her crimson lipstick flecked with glitter, smiles graciously while she stands, as if stranded, in a vast pool of emerald nylon. Her dress, which weighs thirty-one pounds, is almost as big as a float. Even with the aid of three helpers, it takes hours to put on.

It's six p.m., three hours before the festival starts. While the Discus team is getting dressed at the Museo Tematico, a museum across from the Pentecostal church, we've followed Saanna to the Centro de Convivência do Idoso, the local senior center, where the Cardinals have gathered to don their elaborate costumes.

Dancers who will play members of native tribes, kids aged eight to fourteen, are bristling with red feather headdresses, armbands, and anklets. The dancers have to walk sideways, slowly, to avoid crashing into one another in the crowded hall and wrecking the feathers that stick out a foot long on each side. Young girls who'll play the parts of native Flora and Fauna are wearing green leotards and tugging on plastic leaf skirts;

once the skirts are on, adults will help don their delicate, iridescent butterfly wings.

By 6:30 p.m. Cardinal Queen Suellen's three attendants have made considerable progress with her costume. The billowing underskirt is firmly attached, and a cousin is doing up the stays to her corset. "It's actually two costumes," Saanna explains, "one worn over the other." That's because the queen won't have time for a full costume change. Instead, an attendant will peel the upper layer off to reveal the lower one—before the audience, as part of the dance.

That's only one of the feats Suellen will perform tonight. She will have to dance, on high heels, for most of two hours in the equatorial heat in a thirty-one-pound dress. But she's experienced. She started dancing in the festival as a little girl twenty years ago, and she has played the role of Cardinal Queen for more than a decade. "But I'm still nervous and excited, even after eleven years," she admits.

By seven p.m. the excitement is electric. Makeup artists apply paint and glitter to faces already shining with nervous energy and expectation. Off to one side, a girl in the Flora and Fauna group is crying because her costume is too big. She's on her cell phone with her mom, trying to figure out how to make it fit. Her friend circles her with a green-clad arm and tries to reassure her. Men and boys dressed as *piabeiros* are rehearsing some of their dance moves with their fishing nets, leaning, twisting, scooping with the upper body while their feet strike the ground in a Latin rhythm, a cross between a stomp and a ballet.

By eight p.m. Suellen's three attendants are working on her outermost skirt—an astonishing confection of satin covered with jewels, coins, red mesh, white lilies, and white butterflies. The skirt is so wide that even when her cousin leans in on a ladder, she can barely get close enough to Suellen's head to put on her crown of plastic diamonds and rubies and neon shades of colored paper.

We turn to check on the girl with the too-big costume—and yes, the remedy for the emergency is coming, in the form of her mom with safety pins, needle, and thread. When we come back to wish good luck to the queen, we discover that her robes have, incredibly, become even more elaborate: now LED lights flash on and off from the center of the skirt's silk flowers, and her hands and arms are swathed in white gloves encrusted with glittering plastic butterflies and more flashing lights.

We bid her goodbye and good luck. Time to get to the Piabodrome to grab a seat.

Even if you've never been there before, you'd have no trouble finding the Piabodome. Just let yourself be swept up in the crowd. Everyone is headed there tonight.

Like a beach boardwalk arcade, the streets leading to the Piabodrome are lined with vendors. They're selling jewelry (much of it fish-themed), T-shirts (most popular colors: red and blue, and yellow and black), barbecued meats on skewers, candy, toys, balloons, and light wands.

At 9:05 the audience in the right half of the stadium begins waving the blue and red flags Saanna's aunt and her friends have made. "Cardinal! Cardinal!" they chant. This year the Cardinal team will perform first. The Discus fans sit in the stands on the opposite side of the Piabodome, polite and quiet.

The performance begins. A singer in white and green walks onto the floor of the Piabodome, microphone in hand, followed by two other performers in red and blue with tall feather headdresses. Fireworks explode above their heads.

After ten minutes of spoken and sung

The Cardinal Queen will dance for hours wearing her thirty-one-pound costume and high heels.

Dancers for the Cardinal Tetra team.

narration in Portuguese, in come the girls representing Barcelos's Flora and Fauna. They are resplendent in their green leotards, leafy skirts, and delicate butterfly wings, all of them smiling under their makeup as their arms whirl and their bare feet tap out the steps in a complicated dance. Next come the *piabeiros*, in checkered shirts, dancing with large wooden canoe paddles. Black light now bathes the floor, and the costumes glow like the moon in the night sky. All during the performance the crowd waves flags and lighted wands.

At 9:30 the first float appears, and it's breathtaking: a replica of the blue and white church from the town's main street, with a giant toucan at one end and a huge parrot at the other, both nearly as big as the building itself. In the stands, many hands among the Cardinal crowd unroll an enormous canopy, which everyone begins to flap so it beats like a giant heart.

A cardinal tetra the size of a school bus enters the stadium, wiggling and swimming while a team of strong men push him up and down as if he were riding the waves. *"Eu quero ouvir meu cardume canta!"* sings the chorus: "I want to hear my school of fish sing!"

"Car-di-nal! Car-di-nal!" answers the audience in song.

"Eu quero ver meu cardume balancer!" the chorus sings: "I want to see my school of fish dance!"

43

The costume maker Beto Lima, transformed into a shaman.

The Discus team's queen dances in her finery.

"Car-di-nal! Car-di-nal!" replies the crowd. The *piabeiros* dance in a circle around the big float, wielding their paddles overhead.

The giant rainforest float makes its entrance, carrying with it our friend Suellen, her transformation to Cardinal Queen complete. She stands on the back of a hummingbird the size of a Volkswagen Beetle. The float halts. Suellen steps off the hummingbird and begins twirling and dancing, pausing for photographers to snap her photo, smiling for the cameras amid the flashing lights. Two attendants quickly remove the topmost, green part of her dress—revealing the red skirt below. The crowd screams in surprised approval.

Out come the Indians. The shaman, Beto Lima, whom we met in his workshop earlier, is wearing a fearsome mask covered in fur and tusks. Life-size skulls dangle from his leggings. Drums hammer in tune with our pounding hearts. Bare feet slam the concrete floor in rhythm.

A new float, featuring a glistening waterfall, rolls into the stadium. Men in blue and red burst out from it, as if escaping from a piñata. They are *piabeiros* too, holding nets, and they dance the story of how they dip the precious fish gently, gratefully, from the life-giving water.

On and on it goes, at fever pitch, float after float, hour after hour. At ten o'clock Suellen and the Flora and Fauna are still dancing. The narrator continues his song: *"Aqui e nosso paraiso,"* he tells the crowd—"Here is our paradise." *"Viva Barcelos!"*

By quarter to midnight the Cardinal team finally exits the stage to explosive applause, as loud as a cloudburst. But the festival, which started late, is only halfway over. Now it is time for the Discus team to perform.

Men dressed as shamans appear from the darkness in a cloud of smoke. A bus-size float shaped like a *tucanaré* (peacock) bass appears, its tail wagging and its mouth opening, operated by men at the rear. A girl dressed in feathers dances on a suspended platform above a three-tiered float while a mechanical fish flaps above her and sparks shoot from below. A machine blows sparkly particles—resembling glittering fish scales—into the air. Children dressed like toucans and jaguars are rounded up in a cage while dancers pretend to strike them with sticks.

The Discus team's spectacular tucanaré float debuts with fireworks.

Piabeiros rush onto the floor holding nets. A huge yellow boat, larger than an army tank, appears, with a band of musicians aboard. A mass of yellow flags, some crowned with balloons, wave throughout the audience. *"Ac-a-ra! Ac-a-ra!"* they roar. (*Acara* means "cichlid.") *"Acara disco!"*

More than a hundred performers jam the stadium. The dancers spin like whirlpools, wiggle like fish, undulate like waves. The music is earsplittingly loud. The festival feels like a cross between a rock concert and a royal wedding—or between a Broadway play and a fever dream. Molted feathers and LED lights that have fallen off costumes litter the floor but are soon swept to the edges by volunteers who dart out when needed.

Constantly moving, like fish in the water, the Discus dancers seem as if they will never stop. But at three A.M., at last, the music subsides. Performers and audience are spent. The judges won't announce the winning team for days. It will be a close call.

The Goliath birdeater tarantula can weigh as much as a Big Mac.

BY DEFENDING THE RIVER, THE *PIABEIROS* ALSO PROTECT... THE LARGEST SPIDER ON EARTH

It's called the Goliath birdeater, and it's a Goliath indeed! This tarantula can weigh a quarter of a pound—as much as five mice—making it the world's largest spider. Its leg span is wide enough to cover your face.

But is it a bird killer? Maybe not. The birdeater part of its name was bestowed by early explorers, one of whom found it eating a dead hummingbird. But Sam Marshall, the world's top expert on the species, says that the spider probably just lucked out that day and found a dead hummingbird on the ground. This spider doesn't spin a web to trap its prey; like a tiger, it hunts by ambushing its prey on the forest floor—and it's probably not above snacking on a freshly found morsel as well.

"Tarantulas are understudied and underappreciated," says Sam—especially this one. So little is known about this fascinating species that only twice has any scientist ever seen one kill and eat prey in the wild. (One time it was a worm; another time, a worm-like amphibian called a caecilian.) Nobody knows how many there are, or whether their population is threatened. (Certainly, selling them in Lucite as curios in tourist shops doesn't do them any good!)

But here are some things scientists do know: Their bite can't kill you (nor can the bites of any of the five hundred species of tarantula). And they'd rather *not* bite. They prefer to defend themselves by kicking hairs off their abdomen. These hairs get in a predator's eyes, nose, and skin and cause itching and sneezing. These beautiful spiders live in deep, silk-lined burrows throughout northern South America's jungles and swamps. The longer-lived of the sexes, the female, can live for up to thirty years.

CHAPTER 6
FROM FISH MORGUE TO FISH SPA

Tim Miller-Morgan, a veterinarian from Oregon, used to work on beluga whales, grizzly bears, and black bears, but now, on a long table on the top deck of the *Iracema*, he's examining an angelfish who has parasites.

Next to him, Gerald Bassleer is conducting a postmortem on a discus fish. Meanwhile, Christiane Löhr, a German veterinary pathologist, looks through a microscope, scrutinizing some poop gently squeezed from another angelfish. "Many nematodes here!" she calls, urging two Brazilian students to come take a look.

Fish lab happens just about every day on the *Iracema*. It's a crucial component of what Project Piaba is doing. Each year, Scott

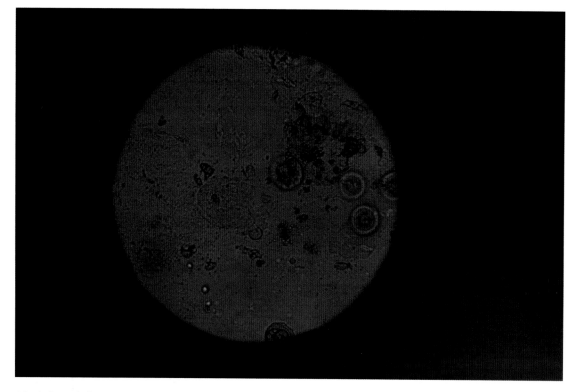

A look through the microscope reveals whether fish are infested with parasites.

At the Bento Floating Fish Station, *piaba* await shipment.

brings together veterinarians and Brazilian students. The vets are "training the trainers," as Scott puts it.

"Gringos aren't the ones to be telling jungle people how to do their thing," Scott explains. So Project Piaba brings experts to train young Brazilian professionals—who will train *piabeiros*—in the art and science of how to keep wild Río Negro fish healthy, happy, and valuable enough to command top dollar.

"These are wild fish, foraging in the river," Scott reminds us, "and we're asking them to adapt to a lot of changes." Farmed fish are bred and raised overseas on artificial food. They grow up in very different water from that of their wild counterparts from the Río Negro. It's no wonder that the wild fish need some extra TLC to help them arrive healthy and happy in home aquariums across the world. "We want to see Río Negro fish go from high-risk fish," says Scott, "to robust super-fish."

He has gathered some unusual scientists—such as Project Piaba's lead veterinarian, Tim Miller-Morgan—to help. An assistant professor at Oregon State University and at the Hatfield Marine Science Center, he specializes in treating diseases of fish and marine and freshwater invertebrates. In his veterinary practice he's used laser surgery to remove a mass from behind the gills of a wolf eel in a public aquarium; he's oper-

Dr. Gerald Bassleer, a specialist in fish disease, and Gabriel Franco de Sa, a fishery engineer, check on fish health onboard the *Iracema*.

ated on a female koi whose eggs were stuck inside her. He has had to tube feed a leafy seadragon (a kind of sea horse) who lost his appetite while being treated for a protozoan infection. Once, he put a contact lens on the eye of a big rockfish. (The rockfish, with bug eyes like a Boston terrier, had bumped his eye in his tank and developed an ulcer. The fish couldn't see out of the injured eye, and so was prone to injuring it over and over. How to protect the wound and let it heal? Tim used Super Glue to attach a soft, blue-colored contact lens directly to the eyeball. As the wound healed, the salt water in the tank dissolved the glue, and the contact lens fell off. Good thing it was blue; that's how Tim found it and knew it had fallen off!)

On top of having all this experience, Scott says, Tim and his colleagues are valuable to the project for another reason. Many of them have visited fisheries and fish farms all over the world. They can share that knowledge with *piabeiros* in even the most remote villages.

The experts and students onboard the *Iracema* have been gathering and examining wild fish almost every day. But today they have a special opportunity. Not far from where we're docked in Barcelos is the Bento Floating Fish Station—a holding station for *piaba* before they are shipped out from Barcelos to Manaus. Handmade from rough wooden planks, it's rather like a big shed on a large, leaky raft. The floor dips, and river water sloshes over our shoes as we come aboard from our canoes.

Inside, a thousand plastic trays, called *caçapa,* are swarming with at least a dozen different species of tropical aquarium fish: rummy-nose tetras, cardinal tetras, checkerboard cichlids, plecostomus catfish, small freshwater stingrays, twig catfish . . . There are other, even more exotic fish here, too. One is called the black ghost knifefish, a species that hunts at night, communicating with others in the school by electric signals. We even spot an innocent-looking candiru, an inch-long sand-colored catfish with appealing black eyes. He doesn't look like one of the Amazon's Seven Deadly Plagues. We'll take this one back to the *Dorinha* to observe and photograph. Keith names him Willy—and when we release him later, we do it far from shore.

About forty local *piabeiro* families bring their catch to the Bento Station, where the fish await an exporter's order. From here they will be loaded aboard big riverboats to be shipped to Manaus, and from there onto planes to carry them to import facilities where wholesalers hold them until they can be shipped to pet stores around the globe. But they may have to wait here at Bento for many weeks, or even months, the way a traveler whose flight is delayed might be stuck at an airport hotel.

Unfortunately, a place like Bento can be more of a fish jail than a fish hotel. "This one's not so bad," says Gerald. He's seen many such facilities on his previous trips to the Amazon and around the world. Depending on the care they received at capture, in the villages where they came from, and at the holding facility, originally healthy wild fish may suffer from overcrowding, injury, or stress and may develop diseases that can kill them.

In fact, the fish at Bento all look pretty healthy at first glance. But are they? A few of them seem stressed, hurt, or diseased—and with the blessing of the fish station manager, we place some of these sick fish in a plastic tub to take back to the *Iracema*'s top deck. They'll provide the trainers in fish lab with clear examples of some of the problems that occur in the aquarium fishery on the Río Negro.

Back on the *Iracema,* Gerald begins today's session by selecting a discus from the tub. Though the water in the tray is deep enough for this beautiful fish to swim normally, he is floating on his side. What's the matter?

"What you do first," he tells Gabriel Franco de Sa, a thirty-one-year-old fishery engineer from Manaus, "is examine the contents of the discus's intestine. Squeeze a little something out, and we can take a look." Gabriel leans in to watch carefully.

Gently, without hurting the fish, Gerald presses on the fish's abdomen, above the base of the tail. "This fish hasn't had any food, so there is no excrement," says Gerald. This fish hasn't been fed. That's not good. Scott explains that sometimes the wild fish are fed only table scraps or fish food that has been left out in the sun and spoiled. Instead, they should be on an athlete's diet—full of vitamin C and protein to help them recover from any stress they suffered at capture.

"So now," says Gerald, "we'll take a scraping from the skin."

Picking up a scalpel, he delicately touches it to the fish's side to sample the protective mucus coating the discus's scales. "Be very gentle, not to cause damage," he warns Gabriel. He smears the sample on a glass slide to look at it under the microscope with 40x magnification. "We'll see if there are parasites."

Gerald peers through the scope. "Ah!" he

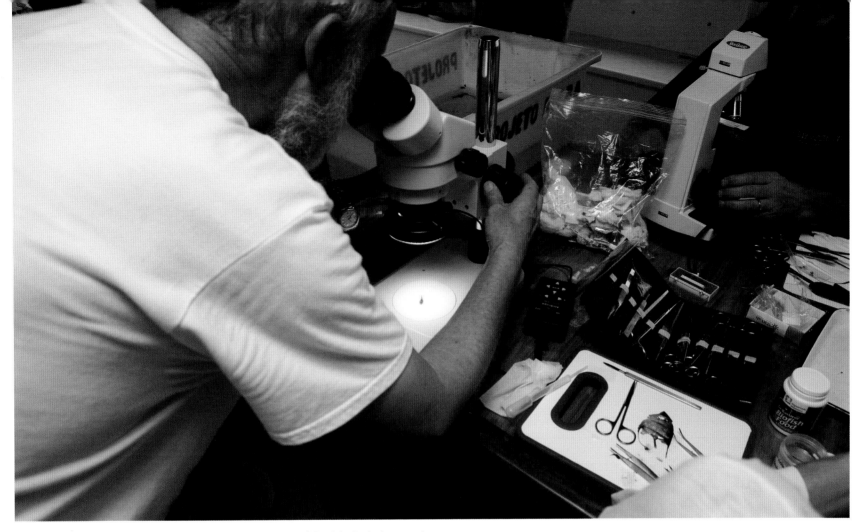

Dr. Ian Watson, an aquarium trade analyst, examines aquarium fish while docked in Barcelos.

says. "A trichodina [try-co-DINE-uh]! It looks like a UFO!"

He relinquishes the scope to his student. Gabriel squints through the eyepieces at what looks like a tiny flying saucer. "This parasite is very, very small!" he exclaims.

"They're *all* that small," says Gerald. Though small, the trichodina parasite can be deadly. "It's in the slime, so it might be hiding in the gills," warns Gerald.

"This fish is very sick. He's so bad he's going to die," he adds. Because the fish is suffering, Gerald puts it out of its misery, adding to the water an anesthetic, benzocaine, to put the fish to sleep. He then takes a scraping from the gills to examine. Gerald peers through the eyepieces. "Now you will see thirty or forty of those little buggers!" he promises Gabriel, and turns the microscope over to his student.

"They were eating the fish alive," Gabriel observes in dismay.

"If you detect it before it gets bad, this problem can be solved," Gerald says. He has authored four books—and has created computer software and apps—on fish diseases, and they list no fewer than six different treatments, ranging from copper to salt, for the disease. In this case, Gerald recommends a bath in diluted formalin, which is often used as a preservative for biological specimens.

Better than treating any disease, of course, is avoiding it in the first place. Fish in the wild almost never suffer from this particular parasite, Gerald explains, only fish weakened by bad water quality and stressed by crowding. "This starts not from nature, but from bad keeping of fish," he says.

Scott points out that it's easy to fix problems like these before they start. "Often, it doesn't take much more effort to make a big difference," he says. As he found in his thesis research, scooping the fish, along with a little water, out of the capture net in a bowl or hollow gourd, rather than lifting them into the air with a kitchen strainer, protects their skin and mucus. Better food, properly stored, restores the fishes' strength. Keeping fewer fish in each container would prevent overcrowding and the spreading of disease.

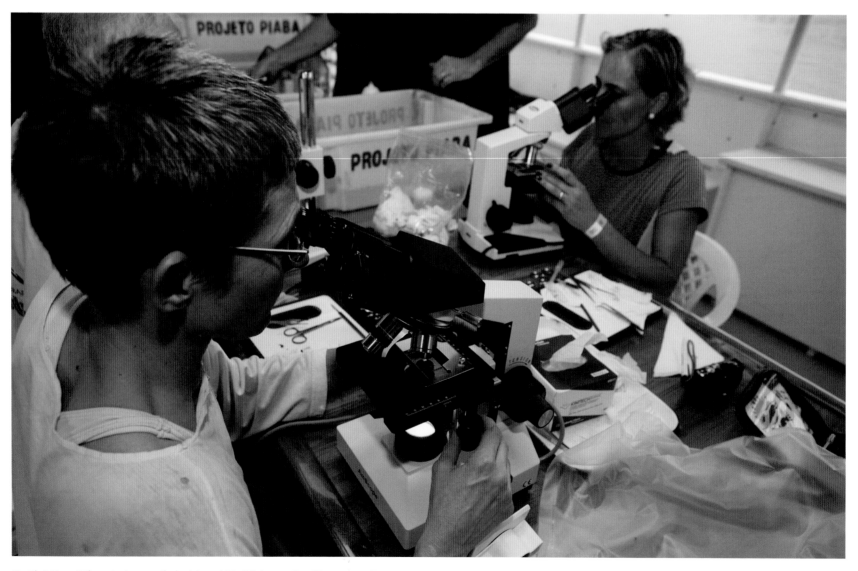

Dr. Christiane Löhr, veterinary pathologist, and Mari Balsan, a Brazilian economist.

And one day soon Scott and Mari plan to transform Bento, and all the places like it, from a fish jail to a fish spa. With grant money and help from the Brazilian government, Project Piaba plans to replace these little handmade rafts with solar-powered paired barges. Fish would be held in spacious tubs with recirculating fresh water in one barge, and another barge, next door, would house a fish health laboratory. The barges would also include a lecture hall for best handling practices training, quarters for workers, and guest rooms for visiting researchers to learn and share the latest information about keeping the fish healthy.

"Now let's try with an angelfish," Gerald proposes to his student. He selects an angelfish who is looking even worse than the discus. The tail fin is tattered. The scales are pale and blotchy. The fish is still alive, but gasping through the mouth, floating on its side near the surface. Gabriel euthanizes it. Then, with scissors and forceps, he removes the gill covering. "Now you will see some parasites and also other things," he predicts as he slides the organ under the microscope. "Ah! Bad gills! Look, please!"

The fish has a gill infection. Since fish gills function like people's lungs, a fish with a gill infection is in as much trouble as a person with pneumonia. This particular gill infection is caused by a bacterium too small to see, Gerald

explains. But wait—there's another problem as well. "There is one gill fluke," Gabriel observes. "The worm is eating the gills!"

Actually the fluke itself might not be a big problem. But, explains Gerald, the wormlike creature creates a wound through which the pneumonia-like bacteria may infect the gills.

Radson Alves, another Brazilian member of Project Piaba's ground team, rushes over to see. He'd been working with Dr. Christiane Löhr at her microscope station, but this fluke is one he hasn't observed before. Soon Tim calls both Radson and Gabriel over to take a look at the angelfish fish he's working on.

This fish has a gut full of roundworms—but, more interesting, Tim has found an oblong parasite called protoopalina (pro-too-pa-LIN-ah) as well. "It's waiting to get to a bird," Tim explains. This parasite uses the fish only as a way station to its favored destination, inside the gut of a kingfisher or an egret.

When such a bird eats a fish infected with this parasite, the protoopalina transforms from a cystlike state, which looks like a round egg, to a moving protozoan, a paisley-shaped, single-celled creature rather like the more familiar paramecium you might have seen in your biology class. It lives and feeds in the bird's gut. When the infected bird poops, snails eat the poop; later, fish eat the snails, and the cycle starts all over again.

Tim is delighted to have found this specimen. "Not only do you get to learn about the parasite, but all these different hosts. It's a whole ecosystem!" he says to Radson and Gabriel. They are fascinated.

"It's really exciting to have this core group and develop the training like this," says Tim. "People are really interested. This is knowledge they want to have. They're hungry for knowledge like this."

Gabriel echoes Tim's enthusiasm. "I love learning this," says Radson. "Always something new!"

The real beneficiaries of the fish lab will be the *piabeiros* whom Radson and Gabriel will soon teach. "If you are a *piabeiro* registered with the [Ornapesca] fish cooperative, you will get this training process," says Scott. The idea is to offer hobbyists the best of both worlds. "These wild fish genes were forged in a hot oven," he says. After all, anyone who can survive in the Amazon is superstrong to start with! Add to that the spa treatment Project Piaba has in mind, and "we're in a very good position to make the wild fish the *best* fish—the most robust, the most beautiful, the healthiest of all. Their cardinals," Scott predicts, "are going to be super-cardinals!"

But only if the farmed fish don't sew up the market first.

BY DEFENDING THE RIVER, THE *PIABEIROS* ALSO PROTECT . . . ANTS WHO GARDEN, GUARD TREES, AND REJUVENATE THE SOIL

If you weighed together all the animals who walk on land in the Amazon rainforest—all the jaguars and monkeys, the peccaries and tapirs, the sloths and the snakes—one-third of these animals would be ants and their relatives, the termites! The Amazon has more than a thousand ant species. The ant specialists E. O. Wilson and Bert Hölldobler have calculated that a single hectare of soil in the Amazon (2.47 acres, the size of my backyard in New Hampshire) seethes with about *eight million* ants.

Ants with heart-shaped heads, ants with sickle-shaped jaws, ants who smell like cedar, ants who bite, ants who sting, ants who bite *and* sting—they are the Amazon's top predators, its primary herbivores, its premier soil turners (far more important than earthworms), and some of the most amazing animals in the rainforest. "They basically run the place," says Alex Wild, an ant specialist and photographer.

Though small, ants have superpowers. Using chemicals in which scents work almost like words, these creatures can signal danger, dinner, and dates. They can lift up to fifty times their own weight. Ants of one Amazon species work together cooperatively to construct complex traps from plant fibers. These traps have lots of holes. When an insect steps on a trap, hundreds of ants inside use the openings to seize it with their jaws.

Some ants wage war; others hold slaves. Some ants garden. One species, the lemon ant, cultivates Amazon cedar trees—by poisoning all the other plants with acid! And then there are dozens of species of Amazon leaf-cutting ants. Using their jaws, they clip pieces of leaves and flowers from trees and shrubs, and holding their booty aloft like parasols, they parade through the forest in long columns that can stretch more than a hundred feet. They carry these pieces to their underground nests, but they don't eat them. Instead, they use the pieces as scaffolding to grow a species of fungus that is unknown elsewhere in nature—and is their only food.

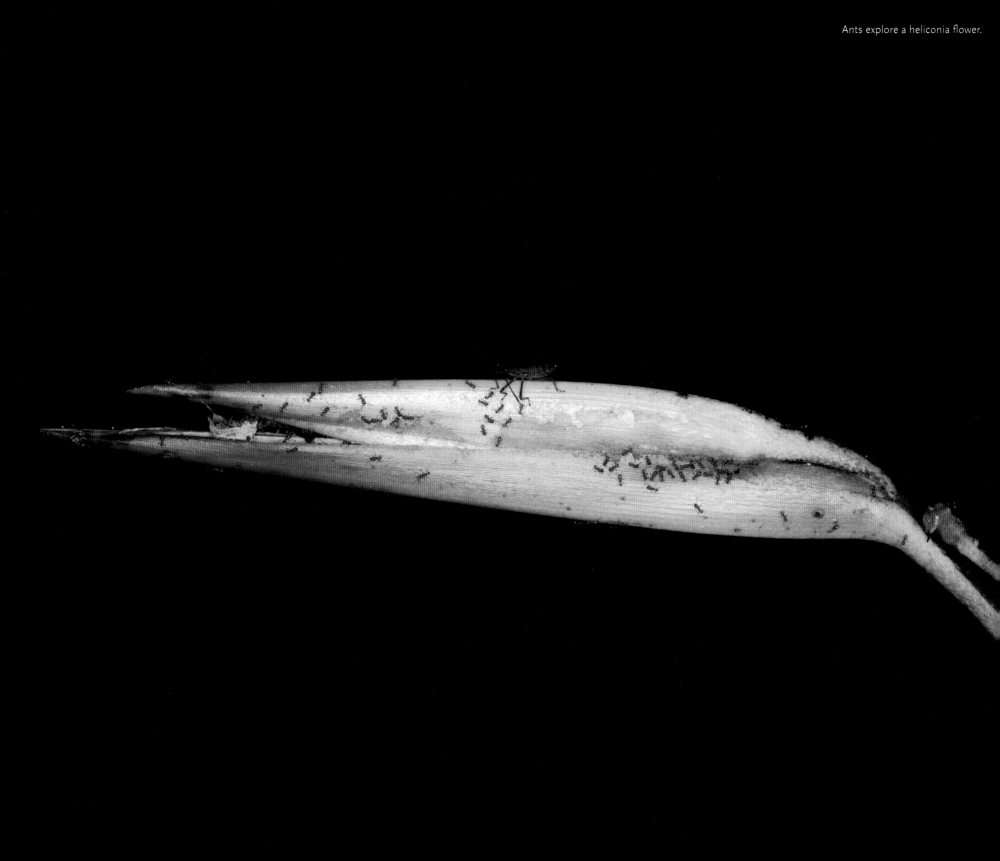

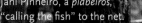

Jani Pinheiro, a *piabeiros*, "calling the fish" to the net.

CHAPTER 7

DARACUA

With a few strokes of their wooden paddle, Jani and Celia Pinheiro's handmade canoe glides quietly, gently along the dark, slow-moving water of the flooded forest. The two women seem as much a part of the natural landscape as the forest itself.

They are looking carefully at the drowning trees and little shrubs poking out of the water, the play of light and shadow, the small eddies in the lazy current. They know the sorts of places each species of *piaba* likes.

There! They reach an area of shallow water, just two feet deep, near some fallen logs. We watch, our motor stilled, our voices hushed. From the prow of the canoe Jani leans forward and splashes the water with her hand. "She's calling the fish," Scott whispers. As if by magic, ripples appear at the water's surface, telling her that yes, the fish are here.

Slowly Celia lowers a *rapiché* (hap-i-SHAY), a long-bowed green mesh net. Using one of the canoe paddles, she herds a school of cardinals into the net and then, without lifting it from the water, scoops the fish into

a *cuya* (COOH-yah), a gourd shell. Gently she transfers them into a woven basket lined with plastic that sits in the center of the canoe. Later today the sisters will take the fish back to their home in their little village, Daracua (DARE-uh-quah). The fish will wait in a holding pen—made from mosquito net stitched into a three-foot-square cube and fastened to the river bottom with sturdy sticks—until a neighboring family with a diesel boat comes to take the fish in plastic tubs to the Bento Floating Fish Station in Barcelos.

A canoe-way in the flooded forest.

The *piabeiros* love their work, Jani tells us as Mari translates. "Every day brings something new," Jani says. "One day, cardinals; another day, small catfish or discus. I love seeing the fish, the colors. This is good work—better than living in the city of Barcelos!"

Back at the village, the houses perch on nine-foot-tall stilts. Right now while the wet season is still young, there's plenty of space beneath the floor of the house for hanging hammocks, storing fishing equipment, and gathering at the table for meals. But at high water, the river literally comes to their doorstep, and the ground floor is completely submerged. That probably wouldn't be a wel-

come situation at your house—but here the people love the river and welcome its water into their homes. They know that their living comes from its wild and beautiful bounty.

Daracua looks like a picture postcard. A boat with a thatched roof rests on the white sand beach. Chickens cluck and peck. There are few mosquitoes, no trash, no pollution. In a five-foot-by-five-foot holding pen near the shore, nearly five thousand endangered baby side-necked turtles await release. They've been raised as hatchlings from eggs dug up by the local people and relocated to a large pen in back of the houses to protect them from such predators as iguanas, vultures, and people. Soon the babies' shells will be hard enough for them to go. The townspeople will release thirty-one thousand turtle hatchlings this year, as part of a Federal University of Amazonas project.

Daracua seems like a paradise where people and animals live in harmony. "This is a special place," Scott tells us as we wade ashore from our motorized canoes. "I love it here," Mari agrees. "I love the people, I love the place."

We're eager to hear the story of this little *piabeiro* village. So that evening at dusk, as we sit together on a handmade wooden bench and a full moon rises over the river, Scott and Mari translate so Jani can speak with us.

She hasn't always lived here, Jani tells us. She was born thirty-seven years ago in São Luiz, a two-hour journey by boat. The people there earned their living by making manioc products. Also called cassava, manioc is a starchy root, like a potato, native to Brazil. It's poisonous when eaten raw, but when carefully prepared, it can be made into a delicious flour, *farinha*, or into tapioca, which Americans make into pudding. Everyone in the village worked—peeling, grating, straining, pressing, and toasting the tubers to make *farinha*. It's hard, hot work, and Jani's dad wanted a better life.

He moved the family to this place twenty-five years ago. "He had come just to visit for a week," Jani explains, tossing her thick black ponytail with a laugh, "but he stayed the rest of his life because it was so beautiful!" He became a *piabeiro*. Soon, other friends followed. Fishing for *piaba*, he found, was much better than making manioc. "We are so happy to live here on the beach, to see the ornamental fish, in a place where the children can play and be healthy." She loves the work of setting out fish traps. Every day is different, she tells us: one day they will fish just for cardinals; another day they'll search out catfish. "Every day," she says, "is a good day when you are in nature."

But Daracua, she explains, is in decline. In 2009, sixty-six people lived here, and all

Villagers offer food to the just-caught cardinals.

the adults (and many of the children, who love to help) were *piabeiros*. That was the last year her father was alive, before her mother—whose seventy-seventh birthday we celebrated at the Ornapesca meeting—moved to Barcelos. Now there are only three families living here. "The market for the fish," she says, "seems to be disappearing."

Jani knows the habits of all the little fish who live in the pristine waters near her village. She knows where to find the shy cardinals in the shadows, and she knows the best places for stingrays and when the angelfish spawn. She knows to avoid catching the fish when they are mating and when the babies are growing. But she doesn't fully understand the foreign, faraway forces that are working against her livelihood and dissolving the community her father built twenty-five years ago.

Jani can barely imagine the fish farms in Asia and America that have started raising Río Negro fish species for export. And she doesn't understand why some conservation groups, trying to protect other fish in wild habitats far away, are working to end her livelihood here. She doesn't know that in other places, wild fish aren't always collected so gently and carefully. Elsewhere, fish for the aquarium hobby are sometimes collected using dangerous and cruel methods—such as squirting cyanide into coral crevices to flush out saltwater fish. In other areas, fish too delicate for most home aquariums are over-collected: the Banggai cardinalfish (a saltwater species unrelated to cardinal tetras) of Indonesia is one example of a fish inappropriately caught from the wild. For every wild Banggai cardinalfish who makes it to a home aquarium, an estimated eight others die in transport or at capture. Justified outrage against these sorts of practices has led some caring people to support a shutdown of *all* wild fisheries for the aquarium trade—even those like Jani's that rescue fish and protect the environment.

"This is my father's community," she tells us—yet another reason why she loves living here. She hopes that some of her five boys and two girls will choose to stay in Daracua and become *piabeiros* too. Two of her sons are in the military; maybe at least one of them will stay and fish. "But if the fishery collapses," she tells us, "we will all have to leave."

What would they do for a living? A few years ago Mari interviewed dozens of *piabeiros* to find out what they might do if they could no longer capture and sell *piaba*

for the aquarium trade. The answers were upsetting. They might have to grow crops, such as manioc—which requires chopping down and burning forest. They might move to a place where they could raise cattle—for which even more forest is destroyed. Some *piabeiros* could find work as gold miners—a dangerous, polluting job that involves the use of poisonous mercury to separate the gleaming metal from other minerals. Some would be forced to leave their forest homes to migrate to the slums of Manaus. None of them wanted to stop working as *piabeiros*,

they told the interviewers, but they had to make a living and would be forced to earn money somehow.

"What is your hope for the future?" I ask Jani through Scott and Mari. Her answer is simple and straightforward: "Just to be happy," she says, "and to remain here."

And now she needs to excuse herself from our conversation. She needs to get ready for tonight's party. The village is throwing a beach barbeque for the *Gringos Doidos*. Scott has been coming here to Daracua directly after the fish festival for most of the past twenty years. The crews of the *Dorinha* and *Iracema* will contribute drinks, bowls of salad, and a cake to the celebration. Today is Scott's birthday—his forty-eighth. When he blows out the candles on his cake, we all know what his wish is, and we share it.

After the party winds down, Scott, Mari, and I board the canoe to go back to our boats. The full moon hangs overhead like a giant eye watching over the little village and our kind hosts. In the dark, I can hear the jingling calls of tree frogs . . . but I also hear something else. Mari is quietly weeping. "What's the matter?" I ask her.

When Mari first started working with Project Piaba, in 2009, *piabeiros* like Jani

were skeptical. How could the market for their fish dry up? And how could joining a fishing cooperative like Project Piaba's Ornapesca help them? Earlier, Mari had told me how difficult it was when she, a young blond woman with a freshly minted master's degree, started working with the *piabeiros*. "At first," she said, "maybe the people didn't trust me. But now the people believe in me and in the project. The people believe and wait." Now many of the *piabeiros* are such close friends that they feel like family to her. She especially loves Daracua—the place, the fish, and the people.

"It's so hard," she says to Scott and me through her tears, "to see this community in decline."

"But that's why we're here," Scott reminds Mari gently. "To do something about it."

Eighteen million households in the United States keep fish tanks. One hundred and eighty million people visit public aquariums every year. "If we just get a small percentage of these people onboard, we can save the fishery," says Scott. "We can save the rivers, and we can save the forest."

Scott believes that Project Piaba can serve as a model that could work around the world. Along the west coast of India,

Mari Balsan.

the Western Ghats is another prime area for freshwater aquarium fish. It's also an area where the forests support wild elephants, tigers, rare birds, and four hundred million people—and some of them could make a living collecting wild fish, as the *piabeiros* do, without destroying their environment. In Bali, communities are now working to restore damaged coral reefs in an effort to revive the aquarium fish industry. In fact, more than a dozen countries are interested in using similar models for their fisheries and conservation planning.

Project Piaba has earned the support of the Association of Zoos and Aquariums (AZA), as well as the International Union for Conservation of Nature (IUCN). "This is

Whole communities of river folk work together to catch and sell *piaba*.

a model program in its importance," said Paul Boyle, the AZA senior vice president for conservation and education, about the project. No wonder: "People taking care of the environment," he said, "is what it's all about!" Richard Sneider, who chairs the group specializing in freshwater fish for the IUCN, agrees. "As conservationists, it's very important that we support projects that are completely aligned with both the people and the environment," he says. "These fish species can protect *all* the environment, and the *piabeiros* play that role and fulfill the same purpose."

Scott envisions pet stores highlighting wild fish caught in a way that protects their habitat by telling customers how they can "Buy a fish, save a tree"—Project Piaba's slogan. He dreams of pet stores like Barks N' Bubbles—where he hung out as a kid—providing a QR (quick response) code on these fish tanks. You could scan the code with your cell phone and link to a website where you can meet the people who actually caught your new pet—and see how they're protecting the Amazon.

But while Scott plans, hopes, and dreams, he also sees the threatening shadow of an alternative future: "If we allow this fishery to be shut down," he says, "we're headed for disaster."

The day after our visit to Daracua, the Project Piaba team and guests are back onboard the *Iracema* and the *Dorinha*, headed toward Manaus. It's evening. At five p.m. Scott and I sit on the top deck of the *Dorinha*, watching for pairs of macaws flying to their night roosts.

Scott remembers the first time he heard a wild macaw, on his first trip to the Amazon. Before that he had seen parrots only in pet stores. "It was a magical moment," he recalls.

That trip changed his life forever. He realized that his first impulse as a conservationist—to try to stop fishery for wild ornamental fish in the Río Negro—was completely wrong. He came to see that the Amazon's survival

might well rest with the survival of the *piaba* fishery. And he realized just how much work it might take to save that fishery from the threats facing it. "I said, 'Holy cow! This is going to take a lifetime!'" Scott remembers feeling sad, overwhelmed, and helpless.

And then he smiles, because he realized something else. "A lifetime. *I* have one of those!"

Fishing for piranhas.

A local senior cradles her team mascot, grateful for the native fish that protect her Amazon home.

BY DEFENDING THE RIVER, THE *PIABEIROS* ALSO PROTECT ... MORE THAN A THOUSAND OTHER SPECIES

Jaguars, howler monkeys, sloths, giant otters, toucans, macaws, poison arrow frogs, anacondas—and more. The rivers and forests of the Río Negro teem with five hundred species of land mammals and eighty different species of bats. More than seven hundred species of birds live here, and more than four hundred different species of reptiles and amphibians. And these are only the ones scientists have counted at the time I am writing this book. Each year, surprising new species are discovered in this Eden-like jungle. By the time you read these words, there will be more.

That makes more than a thousand reasons why supporting the *piabeiros'* work—which protects not only the river but the entire forest surrounding it—is so important. And here's more: The forest not only generates much of our oxygen; it slows global climate change. A Massachusetts Institute of Technology Ph.D. calculated that the rainforest surrounding Barcelos—an area the size of Pennsylvania—prevents the release of fourteen million tons of atmosphere-warming carbon dioxide—enough to fill the Olympic stadium of Rio de Janeiro almost two thousand times.

So these little fish have a big job: protecting scores of other animals, safeguarding the climate, and preventing poverty. Project Piaba "is not just about some little fish and a nerd hobby," says Scott. "It's a solution to global problems."

The Amazon rainforest seen from the air.

SELECTED BIBLIOGRAPHY

Bates, Henry Walter. *The Naturalist on the River Amazons*. New York: Dover Publications, 1975.

Goulding, Michael. *Amazon: The Flooded Forest*. New York: Sterling Publishing, 1990.

Livengood, E. J., and R. A. Chapman. *The Ornamental Fish Trade: An Introduction with Perspectives for Responsible Aquarium Fish Ownership*. edis.ifas.ufl.edu/fa124.

Montgomery, Sy. *Journey of the Pink Dolphins: An Amazon Quest*. New York: Simon and Schuster, 2000.

Monticini, Pierluigi. *The Ornamental Fish Trade*. Globefish Program, Volume 102. Food and Agriculture Organization of the United Nations. Rome, Italy, 2010.

Shoumatoff, Alex. *The Rivers Amazon*. San Francisco: Sierra Club Books, 1986.

Spotte, Stephen. *Candiru: Life and Legend of the Bloodsucking Catfishes*. Berkeley, Calif.: Creative Arts, 2002.

World Wildlife Colombia, eds. *Aspectos Socioeconómicos y de Manejo Sostenible del Comercio Internacional de Peces Ornamentales* (Aspects of Socioeconomics Driving the International Trade in Ornamental Fish). Bogotá, Colombia, 2006.

WEB RESOURCES

Project Piaba's webpage will keep you up-to-date with news, photos, and videos from the Río Negro and tell you about how you and your family might join Scott and his team on a trip to Barcelos like ours: projectpiaba.org.

Do you keep freshwater fish in your home aquarium? Here's a website where you can find pet stores that buy from Río Negro *piabeiros*: projectpiaba.org /get-involved/locator

This video of the 2014 Ornamental Fish Festival was the latest one posted as we went to press. It was filmed at the festival the year *before* we went. www.youtube.com/ watch?v=sMJeKeoEHko. Want to see the video of the 2015 festival? Is there a new one since then? Google "Barcelos Ornamental Fish Festival video" and see! (P.S.: The Cardinal team won the 2015 competition!)

This one isn't for the faint of heart: the first (and so far the only) documented case of a candiru entering a live person's body. Here's a video that shows, among other things, an x-ray of the bloodsucking fish inside its unhappy host: www.youtube .com/watch?v=uWlhRb6fFhc.

ACKNOWLEDGMENTS

For our productive trip along the Río Negro to Barcelos and back, we'd like to thank the captains and staff of both our boats and especially Rafael Strella, our excellent guide aboard the *Dorinha*. We're grateful to our companions on our Amazon adventure for sharing their time, expertise, and company. Thank you Ryan McAndrews; Andrew Murphy; Mike Tuccinardi; Veronica Gordon; Christiane Löhr; Ian Watson; Gabriel Franco de Sa; Adriano Roberto Cruz; James Upton; George Parsons; Gerald Bassleer; Lonnie Ready; Jennifer Sargent; Erica Hornbrook; Leanne Newberg; Lydia Glenn; Eric Rasmussen; Tim Miller-Morgan; Mari Balsan; Vickie Cataldo; Jeanette Whetley; Keith and Jason Spiro; Dean, Emily, and Freeman Johnson; Chuck Doughty; Linda and Keith Heberling; Steven and Louise Heisey; Dan Rabb; Leanne Westin; Marion Lepzelter; Tania Taranovski; Scott, Theo, and Daniel Dowd; Theodore and Gisela Taranovski; Laurel Clarke; and Paul Jardetzky.

Special thanks go to Saanna Lacerda Cram and the family and friends to whom she introduced us at the Ornamental Fish Festival; all the members of the fishing cooperative Ornapesca we met while in Barcelos;

Dr. Ning Labbish Chao; and the good people of Daracua.

We could not have created this book without the help of many folks stateside as well. Deb Joyce, volunteer extraordinaire at the New England Aquarium, largely organized our expedition and helped immeasurably with our research. Kate O'Sullivan edited our book; Cara Llewellen designed it; Sarah Jane Freymann, the author's literary agent, shepherded it from the start; and Joel Glick and Robert and Judith Oksner read and commented on early drafts. Selinda Chiquoine translated an important document from the Spanish. And Howard Mansfield cared for a sick border collie and kept the home fires burning through the worst February storms New England could offer. Thank you all!

A pink river dolphin swims away.

INDEX

SCIENTISTS IN THE FIELD
WHERE SCIENCE MEETS ADVENTURE

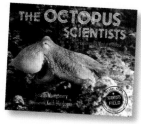

Check out these titles to meet more scientists who are out in the field—and contributing every day to our knowledge of the world around us:

Looking for even more adventure? Craving updates on the work of your favorite scientists, as well as in-depth video footage, audio, photography, and more? Then visit the new Scientists in the Field website!

WWW.SCIENCEMEETSADVENTURE.COM